# BÉLA BARTÓK

## Ten Easy Pieces

### EDITED BY IMMANUELA GRUENBERG

Includes access to online video piano lessons
with editor Immanuela Gruenberg addressing
topics in Bartók's *Ten Easy Pieces*.

All the fingering, pedal markings and metronome indications in this publication
are by Bartók, except for "Dedication," for which Bartók provided no such details.

Cover art by Linda Nelson

Videographer: H. Paul Moon, Zen Violence Films (zenviolence.com)

To access companion video piano lessons online, visit:
**www.halleonard.com/mylibrary**

Enter Code
4491-5168-0141-0184

ISBN 978-1-4950-6117-2

## BOOSEY &HAWKES

DISTRIBUTED BY

### HAL•LEONARD®

www.boosey.com
www.halleonard.com

Contact us:
**Hal Leonard**
7777 West Bluemound Road
Milwaukee, WI 53213
Email: info@halleonard.com

In Europe, contact:
**Hal Leonard Europe Limited**
42 Wigmore Street
Marylebone, London, W1U 2RN
Email: info@halleonardeurope.com

In Australia, contact:
**Hal Leonard Australia Pty. Ltd.**
4 Lentara Court
Cheltenham, Victoria, 3192 Australia
Email: info@halleonard.com.au

# CONTENTS

**PAGE**

**Béla Bartók** was born in the Hungarian town of Nagyszentmiklós (now Sînnicolau Mare in Romania) on 25 March 1881, and received his first instruction in music from his mother, a very capable pianist; his father, the headmaster of a local school, was also musical. After his family moved to Pressburg (now Bratislava in Slovakia) in 1894, he took lessons from László Erkel, son of Ferenc Erkel, Hungary's first important operatic composer, and in 1899 he became a student at the Royal Academy of Music in Budapest, graduating in 1903. His teachers there were János Koessler, a friend of Brahms, for composition and István Thoman for piano. Bartók, who had given his first public concert at the age of eleven, now began to establish a reputation as a fine pianist that spread well beyond Hungary's borders, and he was soon drawn into teaching: in 1907 he replaced Thoman as professor of piano in the Academy.

Béla Bartók's earliest compositions offer a blend of late Romanticism and nationalist elements, formed under the influences of Wagner, Brahms, Liszt and Strauss, and resulting in works such as *Kossuth*, an expansive symphonic poem written when he was 23. Around 1905 his friend and fellow-composer Zoltán Kodály directed his attention to Hungarian folk music and, coupled with his discovery of the music of Debussy, Bartók's musical language changed dramatically: it acquired greater focus and purpose – though initially it remained very rich, as his opera *Duke Bluebeard's Castle* (1911) and ballet *The Wooden Prince* (1917) demonstrate. But as he absorbed more and more of the spirit of Hungarian folk songs and dances, his own music grew tighter, more concentrated, chromatic and dissonant – and although a sense of key is sometimes lost in individual passages, Bartók never espoused atonality as a compositional technique.

His interest is folk music was not merely passive: Bartók was an assiduous ethnomusicologist, his first systematic collecting trips in Hungary being undertaken with Kodály, and in 1906 they published a volume of the songs they had collected. Thereafter Bartók's involvement grew deeper and his scope wider, encompassing a number of ethnic traditions both near at hand and further afield: Transylvanian, Romanian, North African and others.

In the 1920s and '30s Bartók's international fame spread, and he toured widely, both as pianist (usually in his own works) and as a respected composer. Works like the *Dance Suite* for orchestra (1923), the *Cantata profana* (1934) and the *Divertimento* for strings (1939), commissioned by Paul Sacher, maintained his high profile; indeed, he earned some notoriety when the Nazis banned his ballet *The Miraculous Mandarin* (1918–19) because of its sexually explicit plot. He continued to teach at the Academy of Music until his resignation in 1934, devoting much of his free time thereafter to his ethnomusicological research.

With the outbreak of the Second World War, and despite his deep attachment to his homeland, life in Hungary became intolerable and Bartók and his second wife, Ditta Pásztory, immigrated to the United States. Here his material conditions worsened considerably, despite initial promise: although he obtained a post at Columbia University and was able to pursue his folk-music studies, his concert engagements become very much rarer, and he received few commissions. Koussevitzky's request for a *Concerto for Orchestra* (1943) was therefore particularly important, bringing him much-needed income. Bartók's health was now failing, but he was nonetheless able virtually to complete his Third Piano Concerto and sketch out a Viola Concerto before his death from polycythemia (a form of leukemia) on 26 September 1945.

## by Immanuela Gruenberg

One of the greatest and most important composers of the twentieth century, Béla Bartók was also an ethnomusicologist, concert pianist, and a dedicated teacher and pedagogue. Besides Liszt, Bartók is considered the greatest Hungarian composer. In fact, although best known today as a composer, during much of his lifetime he supported himself by teaching piano and from concertizing.

From Bach, through Beethoven, Schumann, and others, many of the great composers wrote teaching pieces intended for students with various levels of proficiency. But the sheer number of Bartók's pedagogical compositions puts him in a class of his own. Bartók composed more piano works than any other twentieth century composer, totaling close to four hundred published works and individual movements.[1]

## Bartók's Style

*Now I have a new plan: to collect the finest Hungarian folksongs and to raise them, adding the best possible piano accompaniment, to the level of art song.*

—Béla Bartók, letter to his sister, Elza, December 1904[2]

Bartók was trained in the classical music tradition of Western and Central Europe. His very early compositions, from his childhood and teens, show influences of Beethoven and the German Romantics, but as he matured, Bartók became more influenced by contemporaries such as Debussy, Schoenberg, Strauss and Stravinsky. In his 1921 autobiography, Bartók writes that three years of inactivity as a composer came to an end when "I was roused as if by a lightning stroke by the first performance in Budapest of *Also sprach Zarathustra* in 1902."[3]

The rise in nationalism that Hungary experienced towards the end of the 19th century became an important factor that influenced Bartók's compositional style and ethnomusicological work. In 1903 he composed the symphonic poem *Kossuth*, about the Hungarian revolutionary who led the 1848 revolt against the Hapsburg monarchy. In that same year, in a September 8 letter to his mother, Bartók wrote, "...all of my life...in every way, I shall have one objective: the good of Hungary and the Hungarian nation."[4]

Contrary to Liszt, who employed Gypsy stylistic elements to represent Hungarian music, Bartók set out to create a style that incorporated true, authentic Hungarian folk music elements into his compositions. To this end, he collected, researched, and codified the music of the Hungarian peasants. Bartók started collecting peasant music in 1905. Over a period of forty years, he collected and analyzed thousands of folksongs. Unlike Zoltán Kodály, Bartók was interested not only in Hungarian folksongs, but in folksongs of other peoples as well. He traveled to neighboring countries and as far as North Africa in his search for true folk music. Moreover, he was interested not only in the melodic or rhythmic motives of this music, but also in the structure of the songs.

Many of these folksong melodies are in church modes or pentatonic scales.[5] Instead of transcribing the peasant songs to fit traditional music notation, a practice that inevitably would have tampered with musical accuracy, Bartók used a phonograph to record these songs to preserve them in their authentic form.

In a letter written August 24, 1918 from the estate of Baron Kohner, Bartók describes the routine of the estate's servants.

> 4–5 people work in the laundry room at all times: they wash on Monday and Tuesday, they fold on Wednesday, they iron on the other days. I know this exactly, because I've camped there a lot, having found a good source in one of the ironing women, who gave me some "fine" songs. Another time we visited the tomato-cooking girls, where I kept on transcribing until 11 at night...[6]

Nationalism wasn't the only reason Bartók turned to folk music. Another reason was a reaction against musical romanticism and his (and other early twentieth century composers') search for "pure," unembellished, non-exaggerated, and objective music. In an interview conducted in the spring of 1925, Bartók said that he thought

> ...knowledge of folksongs is even more important in music [than in literature], because folksongs can be better integrated with music. I mean that peasant music continually inspires the composer. Do not imagine that we are thinking of the transplantation, the assimilation, the annexation of peasant music into the classical music inheritance. No, no. We think that peasant music gives our music its character. Furthermore, if one hears songs from peasants in their original environment, one understands them much better; they inspire him much more than if he were familiar with them only from written collections or recordings.[7]

In his compositions, Bartók created a synthesis between the style and tradition of Western and Central Europe classical music and Hungarian and East European folk music.

## Types of Hungarian Folk Music

Purely Hungarian folk music is divided into three main categories: Old Style, New Style, and Mixed Style. Here are some of the main characteristics (adapted from Yeomans' *Bartók for Piano*):

|  | **Old Style** | **New Style** | **Mixed Style** |
|---|---|---|---|
| **Tempo** | Slow, Poco rubato, Parlando | Fast, Tempo giusto | More energetic than Old Style |
| **Tonality** | Aeolian, Dorian, Pentatonic | Modes, Major, Minor | Frequent major and minor |
| **Mood** | Dark, mournful | Energetic | Ceremonial atmosphere |
| **Structure** | Four lines Often free form: ABCD, ABBC, etc. Six to twelve equal syllables | AAAA, AABA, ABBA Up to 22 syllables | Four lines Variable number of syllables |
| **Special Features** | No upbeat |  | Showing some foreign influences. No unity of style. Typical rhythm: two eighth and a quarter |

In a lecture he gave at Columbia University in 1941 or 1942, Bartók identified three types of settings of folk music. The first type is "…where the used folk melody is the more important part of the work. The added accompaniment and eventual preludes and postludes may only be considered the mounting of a jewel." The second type represents "transcriptions where the importance of the used melodies and the added parts are almost equal." In the third type "the music used is only to be regarded as a kind of motto."[8]

## Bartók the Teacher

Bartók was professor of piano at the Budapest (later the Liszt) Academy from 1907 to 1934. His numerous pedagogical editions, of works such as Bach's *The Well-Tempered Clavier*, piano sonatas by Beethoven, Mozart, Haydn, and Scarlatti, and various works by Schubert, Chopin and others, tell us a great deal about how important teaching was for Bartók. But in spite of his keen interest in piano pedagogy and his success as a performing pianist—whether as recitalist, chamber pianist, or as orchestra soloist—Bartók did not create a "school" of piano playing. One reason may be the fact that he himself had a great, natural piano technique and did not dwell on technical issues with his students. Lájos Hernáni, one of his students, related the following: "His teaching was *par excellence* musical: although he never made light of the importance of technical details, fingerings, variants, ways to practice, etc., he thought the purely musical aspect was important."[9]

Ernö Balógh, who studied with Bartók for six years and edited Bartók's piano music for G. Schirmer, noted that, "Immaculate musicianship was the most important part of his guidance and influence. He clarified the structure of the composition we played, the intentions of the composer, the basic elements of music and the fundamental knowledge of phrasing. He had unlimited patience to explain details of phrasing, rhythm, touch, pedaling."[10]

From accounts by his students, we learn that Bartók attached great importance to the accurate, exact execution of rhythms and emphasized a steady pulse. "He was unforgiving for the tiniest deviation or sloppiness in rhythm. He was most meticulous about rhythmical proportion, accent and the variety of touch."[11]

Like his teacher István Thomán, who was a student of Liszt, Bartók taught by demonstrating to his students, a method that may surprise some teachers today. To be sure, his teaching through demonstration, and his insistence on what he thought of as perfection, did result in imitation, at least among his less-advanced or less-talented students. In addition, Bartók's belief that set rules produce artificial playing may seem at odds with his strict approach to the execution of rhythms and his pedantic teaching in general. The following, however, may shed some light on the origin of this approach. In 1927, Bartók related how, when he first started studying with Thomán, he played like a "savage" (even though his technique was quite good) and how

> Thomán taught me the correct position of the hands and all the different "natural" and "summarizing" movements which the newest pedagogy has since made into a truly theoretical system and which, however, Liszt had already applied instinctively and Thomán, a former pupil of Liszt, could acquire directly from his great master. Thus, the most initiated hands imparted to me the mastery of poetically colouring the piano tone.[12]

## Bartók the Pianist

The piano was Bartók's instrument from the first lessons he took with his mother and throughout his entire career. Over his lifetime, Bartók performed hundreds of concerts in over twenty countries.[13] He performed recitals, chamber music, as soloist with orchestras, and also presented lecture recitals, with repertoire from the Baroque to his contemporaries. Bartók admired the music of Bach and Beethoven, was ahead of his time in his appreciation of the music of Schubert, and among his contemporaries he preferred Debussy, Ravel, and his friend and compatriot, Zoltán Kodály.[14] Bartók performed nearly all of his own piano compositions, some on many occasions.[15] Among the latter are the *Allegro Barbaro*, and "Evening in the Country" and "Bear Dance" from *Ten Easy Pieces*.

## Interpreting Bartók's Performance Notations

Adapted from Benjamin Suchoff's *Guide to the Mikorkosmos*, pages 22–25.

### Touch

- *Staccatissimo*: Indicated by a wedge or vertical line above (or below) the note, it is the shortest possible *staccato*.
- *Staccato*: The duration of the note can range from shortest to no more than half the note's value.
- *Non-legato*: This is the default touch when no other indications appear. The separation between the notes should be almost imperceptible.
- *Legato*: The notes should be connected, but not overlapping.
- *Legatissimo*: An exaggerated *legato*, with slight overlapping of tones. Use of half pedal is helpful.
- *Tenuto*: A weighted touch that creates a stress and gives the note a special color. Notes marked *tenuto* should be held for their full rhythmic value.
- *Staccato-tenuto*: Indicated by a combination of *staccato* and *tenuto* signs. Same weighted touch as the *tenuto* but the duration is no less than half the indicated value.
- *Portato*: Indicated by *staccato* signs under a slur. Similar to *staccato-tenuto* but played with a light, non-weighted, touch.

### Accents

- Accents are proportional to the surrounding dynamics. For example, *sf* in a *p* passage is softer than *sf* in a *f* passage.
- *Sforzato* (*sff*, *sf*): The strongest possible accents.
- *Marcatissimo* (∧): Less strong than *sforzato*, it is a stress "of an agogic, emphatic, espressivo character."
- *Marcato* (>): An accent that is weaker than *marcatissimo*.
- Syncopations are played with some weight and emphasis.

## Dynamics

- A dynamic sign is in effect until replaced by another.
- The second of two slurred notes should be softer than the first.

## Rhythm and tempo

- *Sostenuto*: Suddenly slowing down.
- *Fermata*: Approximately doubles the note's value.

## Phrasing

- When two slurs meet at one note, that note is the last note of one phrase and the first of the other. (Example: No. 7 "Aurora," m. 21).
- The sign (I)—a vertical line above the staff—indicates an interruption of legato between two phrases.
- *Legato* phrases are not to be separated unless marked.
- A comma (') indicates an almost imperceptible interruption of *legato*.
- Rests above the bar line indicate a break between the measures that is about the length of the rest. (Example: No. 6 "Hungarian Folksong," mm. 12–13, and 20–21).

## Szöllösy's Numbering System (Sz.)

Bartók's first opus 1 dates from 1890, when he was nine years old. These opus numbers (started in 1890) go as far as opus 31. In 1894, Bartók again applied the opus number 1 to a piano sonata, only to again abandon this system until ten years later, when he resumed the practice of assigning opus numbers, and this time it lasted until 1921.[16] Sz. stands for András Szöllösy who, in 1957, introduced a chronological numbering system identifying Bartók's works and writings.

## Miscellany

In some places there is a rest above the bar line denoting a hold between the two measures. The length of time is indicated by the value of the rest.

*Sostenuto* means a sudden slowing down, whereas *ritard* or *riten*, means a gradual one.

# TEN EASY PIECES, Sz. 39

*Ten Easy Pieces* were a commissioned pedagogical complement to the *Fourteen Bagatelles*, Op. 6, Sz. 38. The intention for these commissioned little pieces was "to supply piano students with easy contemporary pieces."[17] The two sets were written in 1908, during a period of intense creativity and writing, mainly for the piano. Around that time, Bartók also prepared an edition of Bach's two volumes of *The Well-Tempered Clavier*. In keeping with the pedagogical principle of many of his compositions of that time, Bartók rearranged Bach's preludes and fugues by level of difficulty, as opposed to Bach's arrangement by key.

*Ten Easy Pieces* are easier than the *Bagatelles*. Originally entitled *Eleven Piano Recital Pieces*, the set also included what later became the sixth Bagatelle of Op. 6. After having removed that piece, Bartók added the introductory "Dedication" to meet his contract's obligation of eleven pieces.[18] The ten pieces, with an eleventh as an introduction, are written in a variety of styles and a variety of artistic and technical levels.

*Ten Easy Pieces* and *Fourteen Bagatelles*, Op. 6, were first published in Budapest in 1908, by Károly Rozsnyai. In 1945 Bartók prepared a new, slightly revised edition of *Ten Easy Pieces*, adding clarifications (about accidentals, tempo, etc.) that had not been included in the original edition.

The technical difficulties of each of the pieces are not always on a par with the artistic ones. As a matter of fact, in a number of the pieces there is quite a discrepancy between the two. See, for example, "Dedication," "Painful Struggle," and "Aurora," are not very demanding technically but are fairly challenging musically. Keeping in mind these technical-artistic inconsistencies, here is a list of the pieces in an ascending order of difficulty of *Ten Easy Pieces* (plus "Dedication"):

Peasant Song (No. 1)

Dance of the Slovaks (No. 3)

Painful Struggle (No. 2)

Folksong (No. 8)

Dedication

Sostenuto (No. 4)

Hungarian Folksong (No. 6)

Evening in the Country (No. 5)

Finger Exercise (No. 9)

Aurora (No. 7)

Bear Dance (No. 10)

### Fingering, Pedaling and Metronome Indications

All the fingering, pedal markings and metronome indications in this publication are by Bartók, except for "Dedication," for which Bartók provided no such details.

## The Individual Pieces

Note: Original titles in Hungarian are presented in parentheses.

### Dedication (Ajánlás)

Bartók provided neither meter nor tempo markings in the original edition. The absence of a time signature means that "Dedication" should be performed *parlando rubato*,[19] and the pulse, in this case quarter notes, is the underlying rhythmic factor. This is an original composition, not based on any specific folk tune. The opening whole-note motive consists of thirds that form a seventh chord. This is Bartók's "Stefi motive," representing the violinist Stefi Geyer, the subject of Bartók's unreciprocated love. The Stefi motive appears in other works by Bartók, among them Bagatelle No. 13 and No. 14, and the Violin Concerto No. 1, which was composed around the same time as *Ten Easy Pieces* and dedicated to Ms. Geyer.

Bagatelle No. 13, mm. 22–23

Bagatelle No. 14, m. 9

Violin Concerto No. 1, mm. 1–2

In "Dedication" the leitmotif is presented first as a single line, then obtains richer and richer harmonies with each successive appearance. Interspersed between the leitmotif's five appearances are four short melodic lines that imitate mixed style Hungarian folksongs. All these melodies consist of almost the same number of "syllables" (either thirteen or fourteen), giving the impression of an underlying text.

Technically this piece isn't difficult, but it presents a number of artistic challenges.

- Make sure to control the various dynamic shades and to show the subtle differences in color, such as between *pp* and *ppp*.

- Pay special attention to the above when playing chords with an ever increasing number of notes, as is the case with the leitmotif: from single notes, through two, three, four, and all the way to five-note chords. Have a plan: Play the four-note *ppp* chords (mm. 27 and 35) as softly as you can, and the five-note *pp* chords (mm. 41, 42 and 44) almost as softly, adjusting the other chords' dynamics accordingly. Do not forget that lower-register notes are by nature louder than high-register ones.

- Practice the leitmotif on its own and the melodic interludes on their own, to better characterize each of these different materials.

- Make sure to transition smoothly from the still, level, non-rhythmic, and calm leitmotif to the *parlando, poco appassionato* melodic interludes.

- Clearly distinguish the various touches: *tenuto* (mm. 13–14, etc.), *tenuto* plus *legato* (mm. 15, 23), *non legato* (the leitmotif), and *legato* (mm. 5, 6, etc.). That said, make sure they all make artistic sense by being integral parts of phrases and lines, and by helping with the desired expression.

- Count carefully and never rush the whole notes. This is essential for the proper execution of the leitmotif.

## No. 1 Peasant Song (Paraszti nóta)

The piece is in Dorian mode and it imitates unaccompanied, monophonic folksongs. The opening melody, measures 1–4, is repeated, in a slightly varied form, in measures 5–8. The second melody, measures 9–19, is likewise varied in measures 20–28. This technique of melodic variation, which is borrowed from folksongs, was often employed by Bartók.

This is perhaps the easiest of the set. It is easy to read as both hands play in unison, and there are only three easy rhythmic values: quarter notes, half notes, and whole notes. Pay attention to some of the main technical and artistic challenges.

- Make sure that both hands are perfectly coordinated as they are moving in parallel.

- Both hands should play a very smooth *legato*. Practice hands separately and listen carefully to make sure that one hand isn't "hiding" behind the other.

- Carefully shape the lines, with clearly executed *crescendo* and *diminuendo* as indicated.

- The phrases are of varying and irregular lengths: four measures (mm. 1–4 and 5–8), eleven measures (mm. 9–19), and nine measures (mm. 20–28). Take this into account when shaping them.

- Pay attention to the various touches and accents called for: *legato* (mm. 1–4, etc.), *marcatissimo* (mm. 4, 8, 10, 11, etc.), *marcato* (mm. 18, 21, and 270), and *tenuto* (mm. 9, 15, etc.).

## No. 2 Painful Struggle (Lassú vergődés)

This is an original composition in the style of Slovak folksongs. (The title has been variously translated as "Painful Scuffle" or "Painful Wrestling.") Both the melody and the accompaniment emphasize tritones, an interval characteristic of the Lydian mode. The ostinato accompaniment consists of the tonic, minor second, augmented fourth, and fifth scale steps, creating tritones between the tonic and augmented fourth, and the minor second and fifth. In the right hand part, tritones are most prominent between the first and second notes of the melody, measures 3, 11, 13 and 15.

This is an emotionally-intense piece that requires—and can teach—artistic maturity. It can also teach students that in certain musical styles, even strong emotions are expressed in an understated manner. Pay special attention to the following:

- The left hand's repeated lilting motion is the backdrop of the right hand melody's wide arcs.
- The tempo should be slow and steady, never rushed.
- The left hand's eighth notes have to be even in their timing and in their dynamics. Make sure none of the notes stand out by being too loud, too soft, or not perfectly in time.
- Observe the soft dynamics—between *p* and *pp*—throughout the piece (with the exception for the last two measures), with only slight *crescendo* and *diminuendo* as indicated.
- Pay attention to the subtle dynamic shades. Practice first only the *pp* parts, and when you can control that dynamic level, practice the parts marked *p*, playing them just a tad louder.
- There are instances in which each hand has its own dynamics. To master this, practice each hand separately until you can control the required dynamics, then put the hands together.
- Note that the pedal markings in measures 12–13 and in measure 14 coincide with *subito pp* to create a special coloristic effect.
- The accents in measures 6 and 10 are different from the one in measure 16. The first ones are subtle because they are at the end of a *decrescendo*, while the accent in measure 16 marks the peak of a *crescendo*.
- *Marcatissimo* in measure 19 is louder than the *marcato* accents.
- Articulation: note the difference between measures 5–6 and measures 9–10. Also pay attention to the articulation in measures 17 and 18.
- Measure 19: The right hand "A" should last *and* allow for *calándo* in following measure.
- Measures 20–22: *molto ritardando* and *cresc.* should seamlessly continue the *calándo* and *decrescendo* in m. 20

## No. 3 Dance of the Slovaks (Tót legények tánca)

One of the more popular of the *Ten Easy Pieces*, this piece is in the style of a folksong. The accented downbeats (mm. 5, 10, 18, 21, etc.) emulate the Hungarian language in which the first syllable is always emphasized. The five-measure melody is introduced, in the tonic, by an unaccompanied solo line. It is then doubled (two voices, one octave apart), suggesting, perhaps, a mixed choir. These two statements are followed by the melody being fragmented (mm. 11–12, 13–14, etc.), and augmented through repetitions (mm. 23–25, 44), through the addition of measures (mm. 19, 30), and/or with the addition of rests (mm. 33, 36). This piece is replete with indications of touch and dynamics:

- Note that just about every note has at least one touch/accent marking.
- First, let's take a look at the various accents on the syncopated motive:
    1. mm. 5, 10, 18, 43, *marcato-staccato* followed by *tenuto*
    2. m. 21, *marcato-staccato* followed by a non *tenuto* note
    3. m. 29, *marcato* only
    4. m. 40, *marcato* followed by *tenuto*, over left hand notes marked *staccato*
    5. m. 53, *marcato-staccato-tenuto*, all on one note

  Practice each one of these different accents separately, making sure to execute them according to the composer's instructions. (For a similar treatment of syncopated motives, see also "Evening in the Country," mm. 11, 13, 15–18, 31, 33–38.)

- Now, pay attention to the various touches of other notes.
    1. mm. 1–4, etc. and the left hand part, *staccato* almost throughout
    2. mm. 1, 2, 5, etc., *tenuto*
    3. mm. 52–53 (right hand), *portato*
    4. mm. 47–54 (left hand), *legato*
- Pay close attention to the abundant and detailed dynamics, including hairpins, *crescendo* and *diminuendo* indications and, most complex, different dynamic markings for each hand (mm. 11, 29–32).
- Pay attention to the slight tempo fluctuations (mm. 42–44, 45–47, 52 to the end). Note: *poco sostenuto* in measure 42 means playing slower right away whereas *poco ritard.* at the end of the piece means gradually slowing down the last few measures.

## No. 4 Sostenuto

This expressive piece consists of a melodic line and very original, imaginative harmonies. The melody and accompaniment move smoothly back and forth between the two hands. This is one of many examples of Bartók's love of, and search for, surprising, unexpected, harmonies. More complex and more difficult than it appears, "Sostenuto" poses some challenges, but can also help teach a number of important technical and artistic aspects of piano playing:

- Both the melody and the accompaniment should be played *legato*.
- Measures 1–5 and 33-36: focus first on each hand's dynamics before combining the two hands.
- Measure 11, beat 2: a long *decrescendo* starts here. Since in measure 16 the left hand picks up from the right hand and continues the line, the *decrescendo* should last till the end of measure 17. And make sure that one can clearly hear the dissonance on the downbeat of measure 15.
- Adding to the difficulty of controlling each hand's dynamics is the fact that the two hands play in great proximity to each other, often crossing fingers, and not having the advantage of different registers. Think how you would orchestrate this piece. Imagine different instruments, each with its characteristic color, performing the various parts. Or, maybe imagine the melody being performed by singers accompanied by instruments.
- Practice the melodic line from beginning to end, in one continuum, smoothly transferring it from one hand to the other. Do the same with the accompaniment.
- Maintain a steady, slow tempo, without rushing

## No. 5 Evening in the Country (Este a székelyeknél)

Bartók often performed this piece in concert. This, and "Bear Dance," were transcribed for orchestra and became Nos. 1 & 2 from Hungarian Sketches, Sz. 97.[20]

"Evening at the Village" (sometimes translated "Evening in the Country") is an original composition, not a folksong setting. It consists of two themes: the opening *lento, rubato* theme (A), imitates Old Style Hungarian folk music. It consists of four equal parts (mm. 1–2, 3–4, 5–6, and 7–8) of eight "syllables" each, imitating a folksong. This is followed by a *vivo, non rubato* theme (B), which imitates New Style *tempo giusto* and is, in Bartók's words, "more or less an imitation of a peasant playing the flute."[21] The melodies of both themes are based on the pentatonic scale.

The contrasting sections mean that, in addition to paying attention to a wide variety of details, the performer has to also effortlessly and smoothly move back and forth between the slow, *espressivo, rubato* part and the fast, *vivo, non rubato* one.

- Pay close attention to the notes/phrases marked *legato*, those marked *staccato*, and to the short slurs.
- Make sure to differentiate between the various accents: tenuto (mm. 2, 4, 6, 8, etc.); *marcato* (mm. 1–4, 6, 8, 11, 13, etc.); the piece's only *marcatissimo* (m. 18), as well as accents combined with *staccato* (mm. 11, 13, etc.)
- Pay special attention to the accent in the syncopated rhythm, measures 11, 13, 31, 33, as these mimic the Hungarian language with its accentuated first syllable. (See also "Slovak Peasant Dance" mm. 5, 10, 18, 21, 29, 40, 43, and 53.)

- Note that not all syncopations have accents. For example, measures 15–18 and 36–38. These have tenuto only on the long notes.
- The A part should be performed freely, *rubato*, while the right hand rhythms in the *vivo, non rubato* B part should be very precisely played. We know from accounts by Bartók's students that he often stressed the importance of strictly observing the rhythm.

## No. 6 Hungarian Folksong (,,Gödöllei piactérre leesett a hó")

This is a transcription of an actual New Style Hungarian folksong (see above Types of Hungarian Folk Music). The title translates as "Gödölő Marketplace in the Snow." The song text's translation, below, is from Benjamin Suchoff's Archive Edition of the *Piano Music of Béla Bartók, Series I* (New York: Dover Publications, Inc., 1981):

> At the far end of Ürög village, music sounds;
> Come, my beloved, let us go there.
> There I shall rejoice heartily,
> My love shall weep bitterly,
> Her kisses will dry on my lips, but I shall never forget her!

The chordal melody is marked by a dotted, short-long rhythm while the accompaniment, with the exception of measure 20, is off-beat throughout. The three-measure-long first phrase (mm. 1–3) is repeated three more times: measures 4–6 are an exact repeat of measures 1–3, and measures 11–13 and 19–21 contain slight modifications.

The piece is short and contains many repetitions, two facts that simplify the learning process. There are, nonetheless, a number of challenges and a number of details that require special attention:

- Note that the piece should be played softly. Its dynamic range is *p* through *ppp* with only limited, local hairpin *crescendo* and *diminuendo* indications.
- From the very beginning, the left hand should be played more softly than the right hand.
- Accurately executing the right hand dotted rhythms and the left hand syncopations can be challenging. Practice these first by tapping the rhythms of both hands, preferably each hand on a different surface so that each has its own sound effect. Then, play one hand on the keyboard and tap the other. Make sure, throughout, to tap softly, especially the left hand.
- Note that Bartók has placed special markings on practically every one of the right hand chords: either *tenuto* (on most of them) or *staccato* (mm. 6, 11, 12, 19, 20-21).
- In addition to the *tenuto* markings, there are *marcato* markings on the downbeats of measures 1 and 4.
- Except for the three *legato* notes in measures 19–20, all left hand notes should be played *staccato*.

## No. 7 Aurora (Hajnal)

"Aurora" (sometimes called "Dawn") is an original piece, not based on any folksong. A constant, steady pulse of quarter notes played by either one or by both hands creates a sense of calm, allowing the delicate, often unexpected harmonies to take center stage. The right hand plays almost exclusively thirds while the left hand plays various intervals, and on a couple occasions, single notes. There is no melody and accompaniment here; the phrases are rhythm and harmony based.

- Carefully follow the composer's indications for *rit., a tempo*, etc., for it is these slight fluctuations in tempo, along with the subtle dynamics, that give a clear sense of direction and of phrasing.
- Make sure to show the difference between *molto rit.* (m. 8) and *poco rit.* (m. 13). Practice them one next to the other for ease of comparison.
- Use the pedal as indicated. It is an additional tool in the service of color and character.
- Approach this as you would an impressionistic piece, carefully paying attention to the subtle colors.
- Note that, while the repeated quarter notes are marked *tenuto* (mm. 1–5, 8–9, etc.), the longer note values are not.
- Measure 21: The first beat does double duty as the last beat of one phrase and the first of another.

## No. 8 Folksong („Azt mondják, nem adnak")

This is an actual Hungarian language folksong ("They say: they don't care"), based on a Slovak folk melody that after 1919 became the Czechoslovakian national anthem. An 1853 publication of this song, with piano accompaniment by Mihály Füredi, allows us to compare traditional harmonization, namely, ones that include tonic and dominant triads, with the harmonization done by Bartók, who believed that Eastern European folk music does its best to avoid the dominant triad, thus being open to many more possibilities.[22]

Füredi's version of the Hungarian folksong

An important, recurring motive in this piece is the descending second. It closes the melodic line (mm. 4, 9, etc.); makes up the melody's "echoes" (mm. 5, 10, 18, 24, and 29); and is prominent in the accompaniment. The *pp* echoes are, perhaps, an imitation of how the song may sound when performed by peasants accompanied by their instruments. (Refer above to the section "Interpreting Bartók's Performance Notations.") Note that in the first part of the piece and at the very end, Bartók harmonizes these echoes with very traditional, dominant-tonic, chords. These conventional harmonies follow the unexpected harmonies of the preceding measures. An abundant use of *tenuto*, on their own or with *staccato*, make this an excellent go-to piece for the study of *tenuto*.

- Remember that this is a song, so interpret the *tenuto* markings in that context.
- Never sacrifice the phrase for *tenuto* or detached notes! On the contrary, use the *tenuto* markings to better shape the line.
- The *tenuto* notes vary according to their qualifiers. *Tenuto-staccato* (mm. 1, 2, 3), *tenuto* without *staccato* (m. 1 second beat, m. 2 first beat), *tenuto* plus hairpin on notes under a slur (mm. 4, 9, etc.), and *tenuto* plus *staccato* plus *espressivo* (m. 20). Note, also, the various accents with their subtle differences: *poco sf*, (left hand, mm. 2, and 7); *poco sf* plus *marcato* (left hand, m. 12), *marcato* (left hand, m. 14); and accents (right hand, mm. 21, 26, 31, and 33). They all have to be interpreted in the context of the surrounding dynamics.
- Measure 21: the right-hand accompaniment has the interesting marking of dolce plus an accent.
- Practice moving smoothly up and down the keyboard so you can seamlessly connect between a phrase, its echo, and the phrase that follows.

## No. 9 Finger Exercise (Ujjgyakorlat)

This study offers a very original, unexpected take on the typical five-finger study of Czerny or Hanon. Instead of the diatonic, C major scale, Bartók uses whole-tone scale patterns. In addition, these patterns start on different notes and include playing with the thumb on black keys. The left hand's contrasting, dotted, *legato, poco espr.* melody is marked by chromaticism, an additional contrast—or, perhaps, a complement—to the whole-tone pattern. In measure 29 the five-finger exercise moves to the left hand and the right hand takes over the dotted melody. This way, both hands can reap the technical and musical benefits that this piece offers.

- Carefully follow and execute the detailed dynamics. Note that each hand has its own, independent, dynamics (mm. 5, 7, 13, etc.).
- Different touches are required when the melody is played by the left hand: *marcato* on the downbeats in measures 6, 8, 14, 23; *marcatissimo* in measures 19 and 21.
- Do not ignore the different, somewhat surprising groupings in measures 24–26.
- Measures 13–29: Have a "plan" for the long line of very gradual dynamic changes (*p*, cresc., *f*, then meno *f*, *mf*, and back to *p*). Within these dynamics the right hand continues its local dynamics.

## No. 10 Bear Dance (Medvetánc)

"Bear Dance" is one of the most popular of Bartók's works for students. It is a fast, lively, *perpetuum mobile*, toccata-like piece, with a catchy rhythm, hand crossings, and accented chords. The repeated notes serve as the backdrop for the rhythmically marked chordal "melody." This is a great piece for energetic students. It teaches how to play repeated notes, chords, a wide range of dynamics (*pp* to *f*), and some tempo fluctuations (*poco allarg.* and a *tempo*).

Pay special attention to the many different touches. Refer to the section "Interpreting Bartók's Performance Notations," above, for a better understanding of the composer's instructions.

- *Tenuto* plus *sf* (mm. 1, 2, etc.)
- *Tenuto* plus *marcato* (mm. 5, 6, 8, etc.)
- *Tenuto* alone (mm. 16–18, etc.)
- *sf* alone (mm. 38–39)
- *Marcato* (mm. 53, 55, etc.)
- *Staccatissimo* (wedges) (mm. 6, 7, etc.)
- *Staccatissimo* with sf (mm. 60, 61, 63, etc.)
- *Staccato* (mm. 5, 6, etc.)
- Slurred chords (mm. 69, 70, 76)
- *Pesante* (mm. 35, 77).
- Measure 6 is an example of a tricky sequence because each of the three chords requires a distinctly different touch: The first is a *staccatissimo* rolled chord; the second a *staccato*, and the third is a t*enuto-marcato*. While interpreting each as marked, approach them as individual chords that form, and are part of, a line.
- All of the above touches need to be observed in addition to, and within, the wide dynamic range.

—Immanuela Gruenberg, editor

## Endnotes

1   Yeomans, Bartók for Piano, ix.

2   Kovács, "The Ethnomusicologist," in Gillies, Companion, 51.

3   Gillies, "Bartok," Grove Music Online, accessed November 18, 2015.

4   Demeny, Béla Bartók Letters, in Sipos-Ori, A Performer's Guide, 1

5   Suchoff, Celebration, 2.

6   Laki, Bartok and his World, 208.

7   Schneider, An Interview, in Laki, Bartók and his World, 230.

8   Suchoff, Bartók Essays, 351–352.

9   Yeomans, Bartók for Piano, 2–3.

10  Ibid, 3

11  Gillies, Bartok Companion, 81

12  Suchoff, Essays, 490

13  Demény, The Pianist in Gillies, Companion, 74

14  Ibid, 83

15  Ibid, 73

16  Chalmers, Béla Bartok, 218

17  Suchoff, Essays, 28

18  Suchoff, Fusion, in Gillies, Companion, 126.

19  Ibid, 127

20  Stevens, Life and Music, 328

21  Kroó, A Guide to Bartók, in Sipos-Ori, Performer's Guide, 28

22  Suchoff's, Benjamin. Archive Edition of the Piano Music of Béla Bartók, Series I (New York: Dover Publications, Inc. 1981), x.

## For Further Reading

Antokoletz, C., Fischer, V., and Suchoff, B, ed., *Bartok Perspectives*. Oxford and New York: Oxford University Press, 2000.

Bartók, Béla. Essays. Benjamin Suchoff, ed. New York: St. Martins Press, 1976; Lincoln and London: University of Nebraska Press, 1992.

Chalmers, Kenneth. *Béla Bartók*. London: Phaidon Press Limited, 1995.

Crow, Todd, ed. *Bartók Studies*. Detroit: Detroit Reprints in Music, 1976.

Demeny, Janos, ed. *Béla Bartók Letters*. London: Faber, 1971.

Gillies, Malcolm. "Bartók, Béla." Grove Music Online. Oxford Music Online. Oxford University Press. www. oxfordmusiconline.com

_____. *Bartók Remembered*. New York: W. W. Norton & Company, Inc., 1991.

_____, ed. *Bartók Companion*. Portland: Amadeus Press, 1994.

Kovács, Sándor. *The Ethnomusicologist*. In The Bartók Companion, ed. Malcolm Gillies. Portland: Amadeus Press, 1994.

Laki, Peter, ed., trans. *Bartók and his World*. Princeton: Princeton University Press, 1995.

Schneider, David E. *Bartok, Hungary, and the Renewal of Tradition*. Berkeley, Los Angeles, London: University of California Press, 2006.

Sipos-Ori, Robert. *A Performer's Guide to Bartók's Ten Easy Pieces and Allegro Barbaro*. Koln: Lambert Academic Publishing, 2009.

Stevens, Halsey. *The Life and Music of Béla Bartók*. Oxford: Clarendon Press, 1993.

Suchoff, Benjamin. *Béla Bartók: A Celebration*. Lanham, Maryland, and Oxford: Scarecrow Press, Inc., 2004.

_____, ed. *Béla Bartók Essays*. Lincoln and London: University of Nebraska Press, 1992.

_____. *Guide to the Mikorkosmos*. Silver Spring: Music Services Corporation of America, 1965.

Yeomans, David. *Bartók for Piano*. Bloomington: Indiana University Press, 1988.

The online video piano lessons included with this publication are intended for both teachers and students. They address a variety of pianistic and artistic issues and how these relate to Bartok's piano music. In designing these lessons, I've focused on the most important or most obvious technical and musical elements of these eleven pieces while also aiming to cover a wide range of topics. That said, please bear in mind that due to their brevity, these lessons only offer a sample of the many technical and musical challenges and possibilities found in these little pieces, all of which should be addressed.

As with all types of lessons, you are encouraged to apply relevant suggestions offered in one lesson to other pieces. For example, the video lesson **Legato and Shaping a Line** in "Peasant Song" can easily be applied to the right hand legato parts in "Dedication" and "Painful Struggle." Likewise, the **Touches and Accents** lessons offered for "Dance of the Slovaks" pertain to most of these pieces. You may use these video lessons on their own, but they are most beneficial when combined with the performance suggestions in the Historical and Pedagogical Commentary.

—Immanuela Gruenberg, editor and video piano lesson teacher

# TEN EASY PIECES
## DEDICATION
### (Ajánlás)

BÉLA BARTÓK

Bartók provided no time signature for this movement; the quarter note remains constant throughout.
The fingerings for this movement are editorial suggestions.

Related Online
Video Piano Lessons
3 and 4

# 1. PEASANT SONG
## (Paraszti nóta)

**Allegro moderato**  ♩ = 60–66

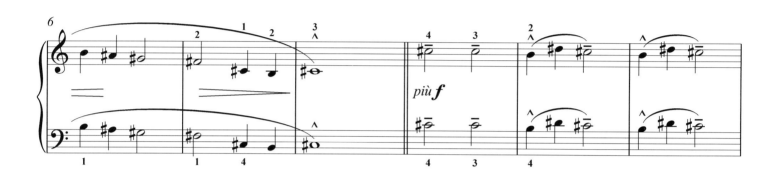

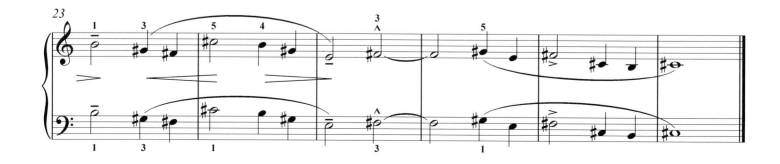

# 2. PAINFUL STRUGGLE
## (Lassú vergődés)

Related Online
Video Piano Lessons
6 and 7

# 3. DANCE OF THE SLOVAKS
## (Tót legények tánca)

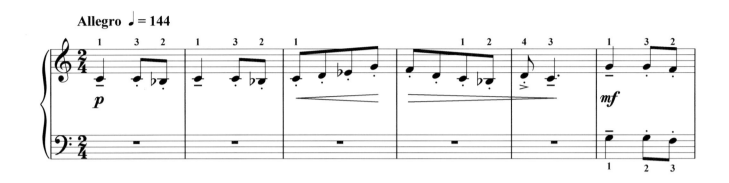

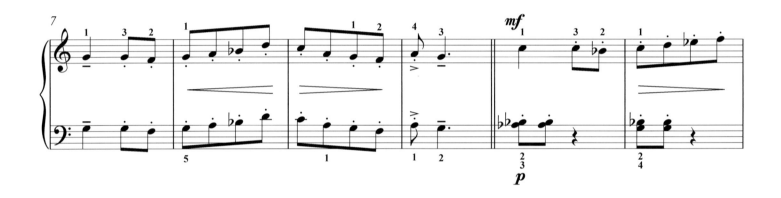

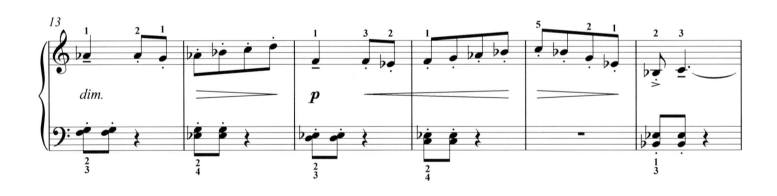

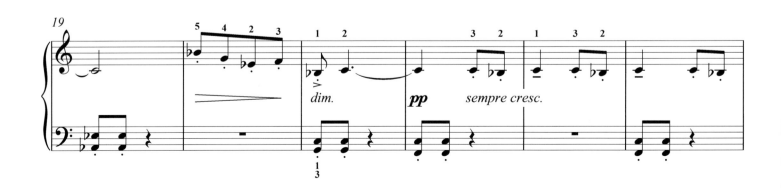

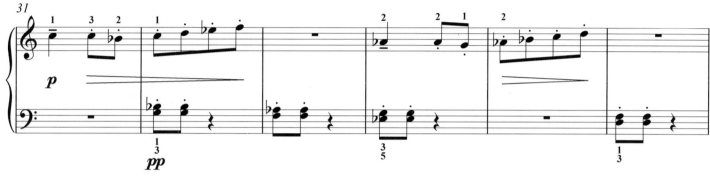

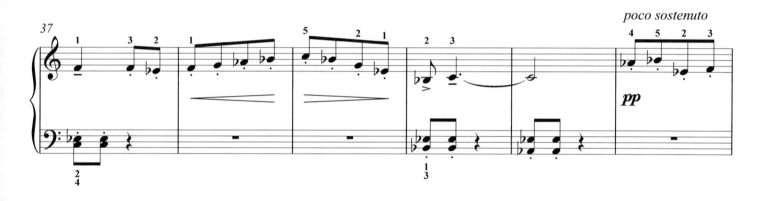

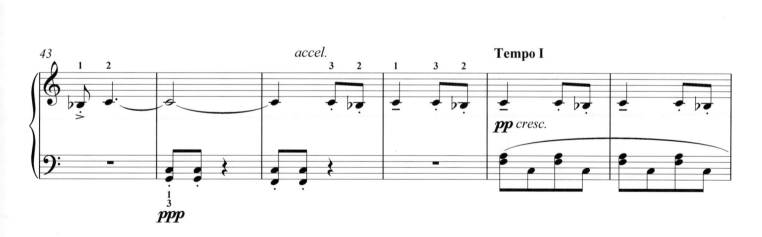

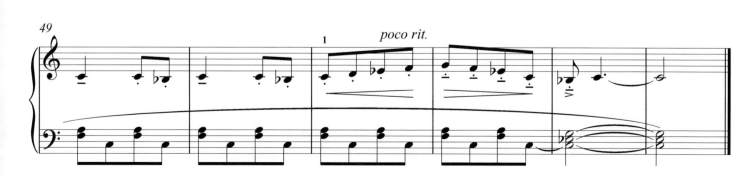

# 4. SOSTENUTO

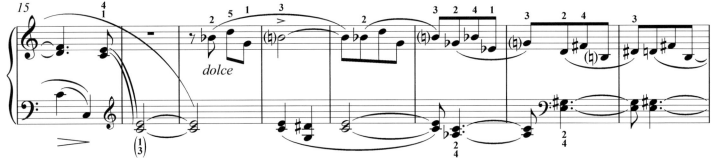

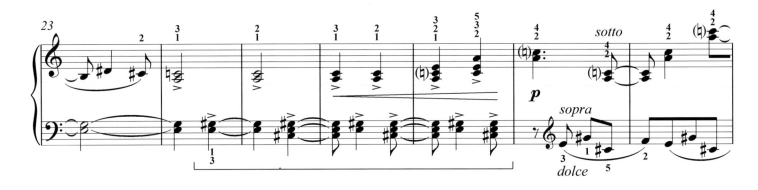

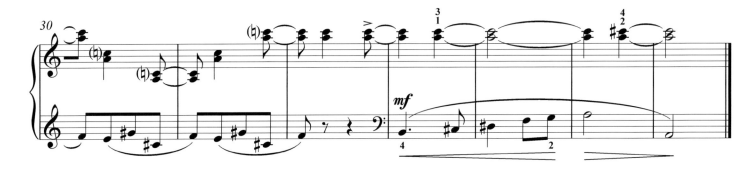

# 5. EVENING IN THE COUNTRY
## (Este a székelyeknél)

# 6. HUNGARIAN FOLKSONG
### („Gödöllei piactérre leesett a hó")

# 7. AURORA
## (Hajnal)

**Molto andante** ♩ = 108–100

# 8. FOLKSONG
## („Azt mondják, nem adnak")

# 9. FINGER EXERCISE
## (Ujjgyakorlat)

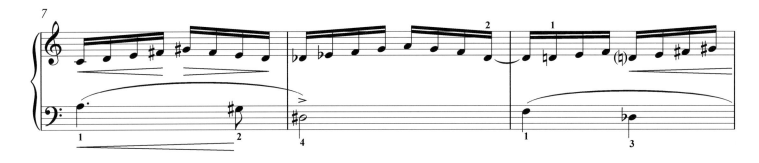

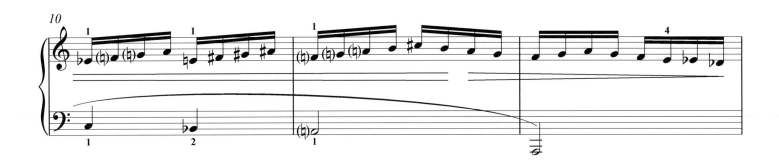

# 10. BEAR DANCE
## (Medvetánc)

Related Online Video Piano Lessons 14 and 15

*Use fingers 2 and 3.

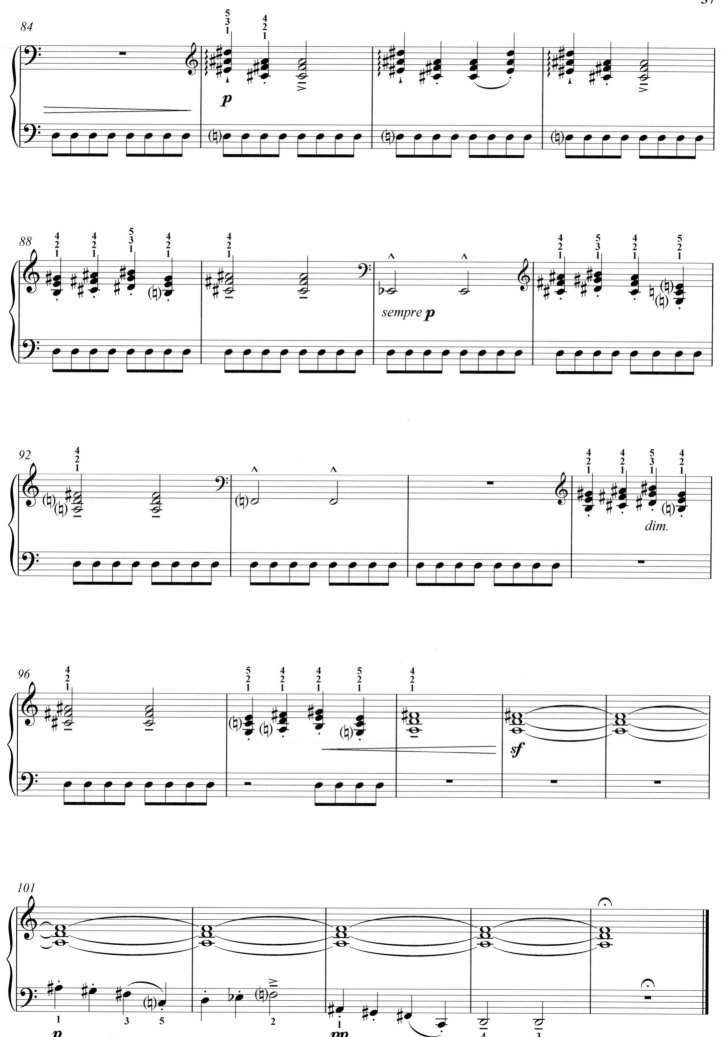

Active as a recitalist, chamber pianist, teacher and clinician, Immanuela Gruenberg has appeared in the United States, South America, Israel, and the Far East. She has presented workshops, master classes and lectures on piano performance, piano literature and pedagogy. Critics have praised her playing as "supreme artistry" (*Richmond News Leader*), "lyrical and dramatic" (*Buenos Aires Herald*) and noted her "delicate sonorities" (*Haaretz, Israel*). She was lauded for her "highly intelligent" writing, "scholarly" and "well thought out" research, for lectures that "exceeded our highest expectations," for programs of "unusual interest" and for having "spoke[n] intelligently about each piece" (*The Washington Post*).

She began her musical career in Israel, performing as soloist and as member of the Tel Aviv Trio in venues that include the Chamber Music Series of the Israel Philharmonic Orchestra, the Israel Museum in Jerusalem and the Tel Aviv Museum of Art. She appeared on Buenos Aires Classical Radio, and recorded for Israel's Classical Radio where she was featured repeatedly. In the United States she appeared on stages such as the Kennedy Center for the Performing Arts, the Corcoran Gallery, the Strathmore Mansion and the Smithsonian's "Piano 300" series, celebrating the 300th anniversary of the invention of the piano. Other "anniversary" performances include lecture recitals in Israel and the United States on Schubert's posthumously-published sonatas—the topic of her doctoral dissertation—in honor of the composer's bicentennial anniversary and a performance of Josef Tal's Concerto for Piano and Electronics in honor of the composer's 85th birthday. She presented lectures and clinics at colleges and universities, for various MTA chapters, at conventions, at the World Piano Pedagogy Conference, the National Conference on Keyboard Pedagogy, as well as for the general public. Dr. Gruenberg taught master classes at the Central Conservatory of Music in Beijing, China, the Liszt Academy in Buenos Aires, for the Latin American Association of Pianists and Pedagogue, and in various venues in the US and Israel. A much sought after adjudicator, Immanuela Gruenberg also served as chair of the Washington International Competition. She currently serves on the editorial committee of American Music Teacher, the official publication of Music Teachers National Association, on the National Conference on Keyboard Pedagogy's Committee on Independent Music Teachers, and is Vice President for Programs for Montgomery County, MD, MTA.

A magna cum laude graduate of the Rubin Academy of Music of the Tel Aviv University and a thirteen-time winner of the America Israel Cultural Foundation scholarships, Dr. Gruenberg is the recipient of numerous prizes and awards. As a scholarship student at the Manhattan School of Music she completed the Doctor of Musical Arts program in only two years. She studied piano with Arie Vardi (for over ten years) and Constance Keene and chamber music with Boris Berman and Rami Shevelov. She also coached with Pnina Salzman and Thomas Schumacher.

A teacher of award winning students, Dr. Gruenberg was a teaching assistant at the Manhattan School of Music in New York, a faculty member of the Music Teachers' College in Tel Aviv and the Levine School of Music in Washington, DC, and maintains an independent studio in Potomac, Maryland.